W9-BEP-256

DISCARD

WE CAN READ!™

Homesick

by Jacqueline Sweeney

photography by G. K. & Vikki Hart
photo illustration by Blind Mice Studio

BENCHMARK **B**OOKS

MARSHALL CAVENDISH
NEW YORK

For Ron the Toad and Russ the Frog,
cousins under the skin

With special thanks to Daria Murphy, reading specialist
and principal of Scotchtown Elementary, Goshen, New York,
for reading this manuscript with care and for writing the
"We Can Read and Learn" activity guide.

Benchmark Books
Marshall Cavendish Corporation
99 White Plains Road
Tarrytown, New York 10591

Text copyright © 2001 by Jacqueline Sweeney
Photo illustrations copyright © 2001 by G. K. & Vikki Hart
and Mark & Kendra Empey

Library of Congress Cataloging-in-Publication Data
Sweeney, Jacqueline.
Homesick / Jacqueline Sweeney.
p.   cm. — (We can read!)
Summary: Ron and the other animals decide to have a fiesta to help Ron's cousin,
a tree frog from the rain forest of Costa Rica, feel less homesick.
ISBN 0-7614-1117-8
[1. Frogs—Fiction. 2. Animals—Fiction. 3. Homesickness—Fiction.
4. Parties—Fiction.]
I. Title II. Series: We can read! (Benchmark Books/Marshall Cavendish)
PZ7.S974255Ho   2001   [E]—dc21   99-058290   CIP   AC

Printed in Italy

1 3 5 6 4 2

Characters

Eddie

Hildy

Ron

Molly

Tino

Tim

Jim

Gus

Ladybug

Everyone was watching for Tino.

"I see something green," said Tim.

"It's bouncing," said Eddie.

Jim cleaned his glasses.

"Tino has red eyes!"

"And orange toes,"
huffed Ladybug.
"I flew right past him."

"Is he from Mars?" asked Gus.

"From Costa Rica," grunted Ron.

"From the rain forest."

"He's here!" yelled Eddie.

Tino bounced up.

"Hola, cousin!"

"Hola, Tino!" said Ron.

"Hola?" asked Tim.

"Spanish for 'hello,'"
said Molly.

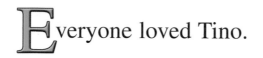

Everyone loved Tino.

Molly taught him
the hokey pokey.

Hildy taught him

"Shoo Fly, Don't Bother Me!"

13

Jim and Tim showed him Bunny Hollow.

Ron showed him Willow Pond.

B ut something was wrong.

Tino seemed sad.

He climbed up daisies.

He hid under leaves.

"I want to be alone," he said.

"What's wrong?" asked Molly.

"What's wrong?" asked Gus.

Tino only sighed.

The friends asked Ron,

"What's the matter with Tino?"

"Homesick," croaked Ron.

"He can't be homesick!" said Hildy.

"I taught him a song."

"I taught him checkers," said Eddie.

Ron croaked, "He misses Costa Rica."

"How can we help him?"
asked Gus.
"A party!" squealed Tim.
"A Costa Rica party!" squeaked Molly.

"I'll bring music!" said Hildy.

Splash! She swam away.

"I'll get mangoes," said Eddie.

"Rice and beans," said Ron.

"Big hats!" said Gus.

"We'll make a piñata,"

yelled Ladybug and Molly.

25

There was so much to do:
sweep Pond Rock
wrap presents
learn Spanish.

Finally they were ready.

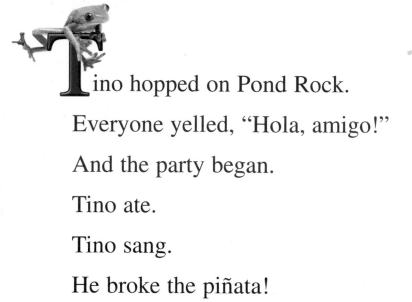

Tino hopped on Pond Rock.

Everyone yelled, "Hola, amigo!"

And the party began.

Tino ate.

Tino sang.

He broke the piñata!

Then he taught Molly the tango.

WE CAN READ AND LEARN

The following activities are designed to enhance literacy development. *Homesick* can help children to build skills in vocabulary, phonics, and creative writing; to explore self-awareness; and to make connections between literature and other subject areas such as science and math.

RON'S CHALLENGE WORDS

There are many challenging words in this story. Discuss their meanings (some may have more than one). Play a game of checkers. Each time you jump your opponent, use a word in a sentence.

checkers	Costa Rica	daisies	glasses
homesick	hokey pokey	learn	leaves
mangoes	Mars	sigh	Spanish
taught	wrap	wrong	

WORDS THROUGH SONG

Shoo Fly, Don't Bother Me! Hildy taught Tino the song "Shoo Fly, Don't Bother Me!" Teach children this simple rhyme. As a follow-up, draw and cut out fly shapes from construction paper. Write a Spanish vocabulary word on each one. Help children learn their meanings with the help of a language dictionary or tape. As children learn new words, they can shoo their flies onto a precut paper Pond Rock.

Hokey Pokey with Molly and Tino. Have children practice their knowledge of right (*derecho*) and left (*izquierda*) through the hokey pokey. Just remember . . .

You put your right hand in,
You put your right hand out,
You put your right hand it and
You shake it all about.
You do the hokey pokey and
You turn yourself around.
That's what it's all about!

30

FUN WITH PHONICS

You can use the hokey pokey to reinforce phonics skills. For example, you can use words such as nose, toes, and shoulders to practice long o words. Or have children form a circle and jump in if you say one of these long o words or out if there is no long o in the word you say.

Long o words:

Tino	toes	no	hola
hello	hokey pokey	showed	hollow
willow	don't	homesick	only
mangoes	croaked	so	amigo
broke	tango		

RAIN-FOREST RESEARCHERS

Tino lives in a rain forest. Now children can create their own. Research at the library to learn about the four layers of a rain forest. Study animals that live with Tino: toucans, spider monkeys, kinkajous, lizards, and vipers, among others. Have children cover paper-towel rolls with brown paper. They can paste on green paper leaves and add vines made from pipe cleaners. Have them make cutout animals, placing them at the appropriate place within their paper-towel rain forest. Children can make Tino and his friends an entire forest in which to live!

RAIN-FOREST FAMILY TREE

Tino came from Costa Rica to visit his cousin in North America. Ask children where their families came from. On a large piece of white paper, ask children to draw an outline of a tree. Add branches. With their family members, they can research their family tree, adding as many members as they can. They might even attach photos and label them. They can also mark each country of origin on a map of the world. They will be creating a treasure to share for years to come.

31

About the author

Jacqueline Sweeney is a poet and children's author. She has worked with children and teachers for over twenty-five years implementing writing workshops in schools throughout the United States. She specializes in motivating reluctant writers and shares her creative teaching methods in numerous professional books for teachers. She lives in Stone Ridge, New York.

About the photo illustrations

The photo illustrations are the collaborative effort of photographers G. K. and Vikki Hart and Blind Mice Studio. Following Mark Empey's sketched storyboard, G. K. and Vikki Hart photograph each animal and element individually. The images are then scanned and manipulated, pixel by pixel, by Mark and Kendra Empey at Blind Mice Studio.

Each charming illustration may contain from 15 to 30 individual photographs.

All the animals that appear in this book were handled with love. They have been returned to or adopted by loving homes.